HOW TO USE THIS BOOK

This book captures all the excitement of a child's birthday, from waking up and opening cards to having a birthday party and finally going to bed at the end of a special day.

Look carefully at the pictures on each page with your child. Read the sentence and then talk about what is happening. Ask questions about the pictures and relate them to parties that your child may have had or been to. Above all, have fun and enjoy the book together.

party time

words by Clive Hopwood
illustrated by Walter Howarth

It's my birthday!

I am three years old today.

I dress up for my party.

I have lots of cards.

Lots of friends come to my party.

My friends give me presents.

I wonder what's inside?

We have a big tea.

I blow out the candles.
1, 2, 3!

We play hide and seek.

Now it's time to go.

I like birthdays!